# THE ENVIRONMENT CHALLENGE

# AVOIDING HUNGER AND FINDING WATER

Andrew Langley

**www.raintreepublishers.co.uk**
Visit our website to find out
more information about
Raintree books.

**To order:**
☎ Phone 0845 6044371
🖷 Fax +44 (0) 1865 312263
🖳 Email myorders@raintreepublishers.co.uk

Customers from outside the UK please telephone +44 1865 312262

Raintree is an imprint of Capstone Global Library Limited,
a company incorporated in England and Wales having its
registered office at 7 Pilgrim Street, London, EC4V 6LB –
Registered company number: 6695582

Text © Capstone Global Library Limited 2011
First published in hardback in 2011
The moral rights of the proprietor have been asserted.

Edited by Andrew Farrow and Adam Miller
Designed by Victoria Allen
Original illustrations © Capstone Global Library Ltd 2011
Illustrated by Tower Designs UK Limited
Picture research by Mica Brancic
Originated by Capstone Global Library Ltd
Printed in China by South China
    Printing Company.

ISBN 978 1 406 22858 8 (hardback)
15 14 13 12 11
10 9 8 7 6 5 4 3 2 1

**British Library Cataloguing in Publication Data**
Langley, Andrew, 1949-
    Avoiding hunger and finding water. -- (Environment
challenge)
    1. Food supply--Juvenile literature. 2. Food security--
Juvenile literature. 3. Water-supply--Juvenile literature.
    I. Title II. Series
    363.8-dc22

**Acknowledgements**
The author and publishers are grateful to the following for
permission to reproduce copyright material: Corbis p. 5
Sygma/© Jon Jones, p. 7 Reuters/© Eduardo Munoz, p. 11
© Corbis, p. 12 epa/© Bishop Asare, p. 13 epa/© Francis R.
Malasig, p. 15 Top Reuters/© Munish Sharma, p. 16 © Hans
Georg Roth, p. 18 San Francisco Chronicle/© Paul Chinn, p. 19
Star Ledger/© Tony Kurdzuk, p. 20 AgStock Images/© David
Gubernick, p. 21 epa/ © Stephen Morrison, p. 22 Reuters/© Gil
Cohen Magen, p. 23 © Ocean, p. 24 © David Sailors, p. 25
© Pool/Reuters, p. 26 © Pool/Reuters, p. 27 Reuters/© Ismael
Abdi, p. 34 © David Howells, p. 35 AgStock Image/© Bill
Barksdale, p. 38 © Jane Hahn, p. 39 © Rick D'Elia; Corbis
Sygma p. 15 bottom © Pierre Vauthey; Getty Images p. 9
America 24-7/Arthur Pollock, p. 10 Cate Gillon, p. 30 AFP
Photo/Peter Martell p. 32 Gallo Images/Travel Ink, p. 36 AFP
Photo/Peter Parks; iStockphoto.com p. 17 © Wrangel, p. 28
© RedHelga, p. 29 © Bartosz Hadyniak, p. 41 © Amanda
Grandfield; Shutterstock p. 6 © Mosista Pambudi, p. 37 © Gail
Johnson.

Cover photograph of a South African girl drinking water from
a communal tap (one of three taps serving a community of
nearly 2,000 people) is reproduced with permission of Corbis
epa/© Jon Hursa.

We would like to thank Michael D. Mastrandrea, Ph.D. for his
invaluable help in the preparation of this book.

**Disclaimer**
All the internet addresses (URLs) given in this book were valid
at the time of going to press. However, due to the dynamic
nature of the internet, some addresses may have changed, or
sites may have changed or ceased to exist since publication.
While the author and publisher regret any inconvenience this
may cause readers, no responsibility for any such changes can
be accepted by either the author or the publisher.

D

Books are to be returned on or before
the last date below.

LIBREX-

# Contents

Words appearing in the text in bold, **like this**, are explained in the glossary.

# Famine and drought

Have you ever been really hungry? Real hunger is not just going without food for a few hours. It means never having enough food for periods of weeks, months, or even years. And have you ever been thirsty? Imagine never being able to quench your thirst, with no tap to turn on and no bottle to drink from.

### What's the point of food?

Everybody eats food. We need it to stay alive. If we do not eat, our bodies will not be able to operate. Food gives us the energy to do work. It also gives us the **nutrients** that allow us to grow and stay healthy.

Where does food come from? Most of it is taken from plants or animals. We grow crop plants such as grains, fruits, and vegetables. We raise animals, including cattle, pigs, and sheep, so that we can eat their meat. We also eat other animal products, such as eggs and milk.

## A hungry world

Across the world, huge numbers of people go hungry and thirsty. Without enough healthy food, these people's bodies will never grow or fight disease properly. They will be **malnourished**, meaning they lack essential **nutrition**, and many people will die. People can also die from lack of clean water. Here are some figures relating to hunger.

- The total **population** (number of people) in the world is about 6.9 billion.

- Over 872 million people do not have enough food. Over 60 per cent of these people are women.

- Every minute, ten children die due to lack of proper food.

- Over one billion people do not have access to safe drinking water.

*Millions of the world's population do not have enough food or water. The darker red areas on this map mark the worst affected places.*

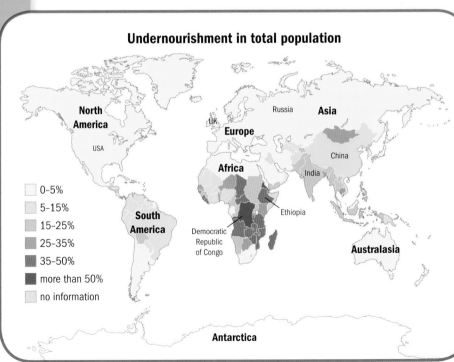

**Undernourishment in total population**

- 0–5%
- 5–15%
- 15–25%
- 25–35%
- 35–50%
- more than 50%
- no information

North America

USA

South America

UK

Europe

Russia

Asia

China

India

Africa

Ethiopia

Democratic Republic of Congo

Australasia

Antarctica

## Your opinion counts

Mass food and water shortages are global tragedies. But in some areas of the world these problems could get worse. This is because the world's climate is changing. This is affecting the amount of rainfall we get, which alters the way we grow food and access water. These changes will affect us all, wherever we live.

How can governments and farmers make sure there is enough for everyone? What choices are there? This book will help you explore these challenges. It will also help you make your own decisions about how to make sure everyone has enough healthy food to eat and clean water to drink. Everyone is affected by these issues, so your opinion matters!

Young children like this Somalian child suffer most from lack of nutrition.

**WORD BANK**

| | |
|---|---|
| **malnourished** | lacking essential nutrients in one's diet, which results in disease and other difficulties |
| **nutrient** | substance in food that supports health and growth |
| **nutrition** | consumption of food that helps bodies to grow and replace their tissues (such as bone) |
| **population** | total number of people in an area |

## Looking for evidence

How can you find out more about the future of food and water shortages? To make a balanced judgement, you need evidence – facts, figures, images, and expert views. Here are some places to look:

- Libraries have books of all kinds, as well as DVDs and databases of information such as news articles.

- The internet offers a huge choice of sites about food, **agriculture** (farming), and water supplies.

- Newspapers, radio, and television often have stories about food.

- Other people may have views and experiences that will help you understand the subject.

## What causes famine and drought?

Since 1976 the countries of the **United Nations (UN)** have recognized that all the people in the world have a fundamental right to be free from hunger. Governments and charities work hard to provide food and water aid to areas that need it.

All the same, many millions of people still go hungry or even die because of lack of food and water. These are the major causes.

- *Poverty*: People cannot afford food.

- *Crop failure:* Not enough food can be grown.

- *Politics:* Governments fail to get food to their people.

- *War:* **Refugees** flee from violence and have no food.

- *Natural disasters:* Floods, earthquakes, and **drought** (lack of water) destroy supplies.

Rice is the most important food for most people in East Asia. If the crop does not grow well, many may go hungry.

# Famine in Haiti

## Poor Haitians Resort to Eating Dirt
### by Jonathan M. Katz

Port-au-Prince, Haiti – It was lunchtime in one of Haiti's worst slums, and Charlene Dumas was eating mud ...

Charlene, 16, has come to rely on a traditional Haitian remedy for hunger pangs: cookies made of dried yellow dirt from the country's central plateau ... Cookies made of dirt, salt, and vegetable shortening have become a regular meal.

'When my mother does not cook anything, I have to eat them three times a day,' Charlene said.

This news story published by the Associated Press on 30 January 2008 shows how terrible hunger can get. A girl named Charlene shows the desperate measures people take:

Huge numbers of Haiti's poor have been forced to eat mud like this because of severe food shortages. There are several causes. As an island, Haiti has to import most of its food, meaning it must have it transported from other places. But world food prices have shot up, and few people in Haiti can afford it. Haiti's own crops are often ruined by floods and hurricanes. (You can read the full story at: http://news.nationalgeographic.com/news/2008/01/080130-AP-haiti-eatin.html.)

A woman puts mud pies out to bake in the Sun during the 2008 famine in Haiti.

**WORD BANK**

| | |
|---|---|
| **agriculture** | farming |
| **drought** | severe and long-lasting lack of water in a region |
| **poverty** | state of being poor, with little money and few ways to support oneself |
| **refugee** | person forced to leave his or her home, because of war or natural disaster |

# Too many mouths to feed

There are an awful lot of people in the world – and all of them need food and water. Earth's **population** has grown with amazing speed. Back in 1950, there were about 2.5 billion of us. By 2010 the total had shot up to 6.9 billion people. By 2025 some experts estimate it will reach 8.5 billion people, and 9.2 billion by 2050.

## More people, more food

Why has there been such a massive increase? The answer is simple: until recently the birth rate had been rising, and the death rate has been falling. This is partly because medicine and health have improved hugely, meaning that people live longer. However, the figures below show that the speed of population growth is now slowing down.

Today, about 12 per cent of the world's people do not get enough to eat. This problem is likely to grow in years to come as the global population increases.

This graph shows how the world's population has increased over the last 200 years. Look at the figures carefully. What do they tell you about the speed of that growth? What would the graph look like if you added the estimated figures for 2025 and 2050?

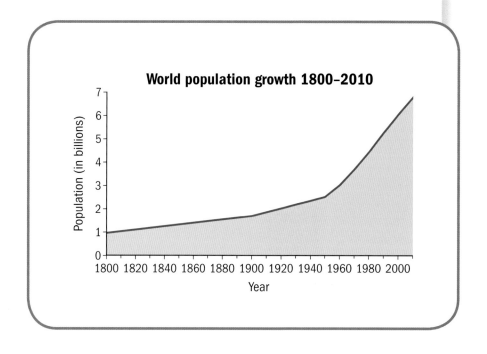

**World population growth 1800–2010**

# Population growth in Burkina Faso and the UK

The story on the right is about Burkina Faso, a **developing country** in Africa. The story below is about the United Kingdom, a **developed country** in Europe.

Both of these stories are about population growth. Which country do you think has the fastest-growing population? It is hard to tell from the reports. In fact, Burkina Faso has one of the highest growth rates in the world (3.10 per cent a year). The United Kingdom has one of the lowest (0.28 per cent).

## Burkina Faso: Population Growth Outstrips Economic Gains

Ouagadougou, Burkina Faso – (Burkina Faso's) population is growing at 3.1 percent a year, or more than 400,000 people ... Burkina Faso's population nearly tripled over 30 years to more than 14 million people as of 2006 ... Population growth is cancelling out benefits from the country's 2008 five-percent economic growth.

(You can read the full story, which was published on 21 January 2009, by IRIN, a **UN** news organization, at www.irinnews.org/Report.aspx?ReportId=82501.)

## Birth Rate Pushes UK Population to Greatest Increase in Almost 50 Years by Sam Jones

London – The UK experienced its greatest population increase in almost half a century last year, with a baby boom pushing the number of people living in the country above 61 million for the first time ...

There were 408,000 more people in Britain in 2008 than in the previous year. The overall population has risen by 2 million since 2001, to a peak of 61.4 million.

(You can read the full story, which was published on 27 August 2009, in the *Guardian,* at www.guardian.co.uk/world/2009/aug/27/population-growth-uk-birth-rate-immigration.)

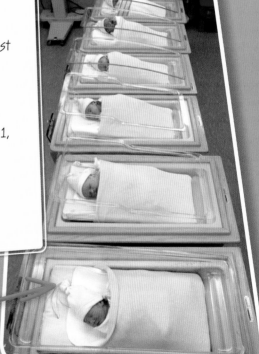

More than 240 babies are born throughout the world every minute.

**WORD BANK**

| | |
|---|---|
| **developed country** | country that manages its money, goods, and trade in a stable way |
| **developing country** | country that does not yet manage its money, goods, and trade in a stable way |
| **United Nations (UN)** | organization of different countries that formed in 1945 to promote |

## Famine throughout the world

We are used to seeing **famine** (extreme food shortages) take place in developing countries, especially in Africa or South East Asia. Yet, over the last 1,000 years, hunger and famine have struck in many different parts of the world. For example:

| Year | Country |
|------|---------|
| 1005 | England |
| 1199 | Egypt |
| 1231 | Japan |
| 1345 | India |
| 1441 | Mexico |
| 1504 | Spain |
| 1660 | Poland |
| 1783 | Iceland |
| 1845 | Ireland |
| 1946 | Russia |

## Rural and urban

Do you live in a **rural** (countryside) area? Or do you live in an **urban** (city) area? If you live in an urban area, you are now part of a global majority. In 2007 the number of urban dwellers in the world overtook the number of rural dwellers – for the first time in history. Experts predict there will be five billion people living in urban areas by 2030.

This change is bound to have a big effect on our supplies of food and water. For a start, it means less land for farming. Cities will have to make room for their growing populations by building on areas that are currently undeveloped. These large urban areas will also be vulnerable to food shortages. If food cannot be brought in, these areas will run out of supplies for their large populations in a very short time.

In many parts of the world, cities are quickly expanding into the countryside nearby.

## How to think critically

When you start looking for information about the global food supply, you will find huge amounts of evidence. It is easy to get confused. So, how do you decide what is useful? What evidence can you trust? Here are some questions to remember to ask yourself. They will help you to think critically about what you find.

- Is this a real fact, or just somebody's opinion?

- Does it come from a source you can rely on?

- Have you looked at two different accounts or sets of figures to get a well-rounded view?

- Are you thinking objectively (without favouring one side) in your research – or are you just trying to prove a point?

*A poor family digs desperately for potatoes during the famine in Ireland during the 1840s. Nearly one million people died during the famine.*

## How much food is there?

Research shows that there is enough food available to give every person on the planet over 2 kilogrammes (4 pounds) of food every day. This includes vegetables, fruits, grains, meat, and fish.

But, sadly, huge numbers of people never get their share of the food. One major reason is **poverty**: they have no money to buy it with. Another is **distribution**: the food is not shared fairly. Some people get a lot more, some get less, and some get none at all. This is the central problem of world hunger.

## What is food security?

There is probably food in your house. If you run out, somebody can go to a shop and buy more. The food will also probably be good for you, with the **nutrients** we all need to stay healthy. This means you have a safe source of food, or **food security**.

But what happens if there is no food? Suppose the shop was empty – or you had no nearby shop at all. Suppose no food came to your region, and the crops failed to grow. You would not have a safe source of food. Millions of people throughout the world have no food security, and so they live in fear of starvation.

Food shortages in Zimbabwe in 2007 led to empty shelves in the shops.

## Poverty and hunger

There are many major causes of hunger. But experts agree that the biggest of these causes is poverty. Very poor people do not have the money to buy food – even if it is available. Lack of food means they are probably weak, **malnourished**, and likely to become seriously sick. This means they are unable to work, go to school, learn skills, or care for each other.

You can see that poverty and hunger are part of a cycle. One leads to the other, and it is almost impossible to break out of the cycle. Hungry people often give birth to weak children, who themselves are likely to be poor. Poverty is the first problem that must be tackled if we want to get rid of world hunger.

Lack of water makes the ground hard to cultivate. Little food will grow in this poor soil.

## What would YOU do ?

If poverty is the biggest problem causing world hunger, what is the solution? Politicians and charities have tried many different ways to meet this challenge – more money, more food, more investment in **industry**, more supplies, and more help and advice for farmers. These have all had huge effects, but the problems have not gone away.

Find out more about the causes of hunger and poverty. Begin by looking at the websites of the UN's Food and **Agriculture** Organization, or FAO (www. fao.org), and the UN's World Food Program (www.wfp.org). Then decide what you would do to break the poverty cycle.

**WORD BANK**

**distribution**   spreading or delivering of something over a wide area
**food security**   having a reliable food source
**industry**   type of work that creates something to be sold, often through the use of factories and power plants

# Growing food

Farming is the oldest **industry** in the world. It is also one of the biggest. Today, farms of all sorts cover more than one-third of the world's land area. You could also say that farming is the most important human activity. Without the food grown on farms, we would all starve.

## Feeding an expanding world

In the past 100 years, the job of feeding the world has become harder. As we have seen, this is because the global **population** has been increasing rapidly. Much more food has to be grown to meet the rising demand. How has this been done?

### Global growth

This chart shows the rise in the world's production of major food crops in the past 50 years:

| Food | 1961 output (in millions of tonnes) | 2008 output (in millions of tonnes) |
|------|-------------------------------------|-------------------------------------|
| Rice | 215.6 | 685.0 |
| Wheat | 222.3 | 689.9 |
| Maize | 205.0 | 822.7 |
| Barley | 72.4 | 157.6 |
| Meat | 71.3 | 279.9 |

Do you want to find out more? Go to the statistics website of the **UN**'s Food and Agriculture Organization at http://faostat.fao.org/site/339/default.aspx.

Farmers, helped by scientists, have found many new ways to produce crops of meat, grains, vegetables, and other things (see the Green Revolution case study opposite). This has had an amazing effect on the supply of food. In fact, in the last 50 years, the world's output of **agriculture** has grown even faster than the world's population.

'Why should there be hunger and deprivation in any land, in any city, at any table, when man has the resources and the scientific know-how to provide all mankind with the basic necessities of life?'

**Martin Luther King, Jr., civil rights campaigner, 1964**

# The Green Revolution

The great jump in farm production since World War II (1939–45) has been called the Green Revolution. It began in the 1940s, when scientists developed new varieties of grain crops, such as rice and wheat. These grew more quickly than the old ones and gave a greater **yield** (amount of food produced).

Farmers in India, China, and other **developing countries** sowed the new varieties. They helped the crops grow fast by spreading new chemical **fertilizers**. They used new, powerful sprays called **pesticides** and **herbicides** to kill pests, weeds, and plant diseases. The results were dramatic. Regions that had been threatened by **famine** suddenly had bumper (unusually large) harvests.

New chemical sprays keep down weeds and pests and help bigger crops to grow.

Scientists grow new varieties of plants in a laboratory in France.

**WORD BANK**

| | |
|---|---|
| **fertilizer** | special material spread on the ground to help plants grow better |
| **herbicide** | chemical that is sprayed on the ground to destroy unwanted plants (such as weeds) |
| **pesticide** | chemical that is sprayed on the ground to destroy animal and insect pests that harm crops |

## Crops we cannot eat

Do farmers just grow food? Not these days. Many modern crops are not for us to eat. Special plants such as elephant grass are grown simply to make fuels called **biofuels**. They can be burned in a power station or processed into a kind of diesel for vehicles. Other crops, such as soybeans and rapeseed, are mainly for feeding cattle.

The world needs fuel and meat. But is this a sensible way of getting them? Most people would say that food is more important than fuel. Elephant grass and soybeans use up farmland that could be used for growing human food. What do you think?

## But can we go on like this?

The new farming methods that powered the Green Revolution (see page 15) seemed like a huge success. They gave **food security** to a lot more people. But the new techniques and materials created problems as well – most of them involving the environment. Today, these problems have got bigger.

Here are some of the ways in which the Green Revolution may affect the food supply in future years:

- *Use of **fossil fuels**:* Farms need huge amounts of fuels (to run machinery) and fertilizers (to help plants grow). Both use a lot of fossil fuels (oil and natural gas), which are quickly running out. Burning fossil fuels to create energy causes major problems for the environment as well (see page 33).

- *Destruction of the rainforest:* Large areas of unspoiled wilderness are being plowed up so that food can be grown for cattle.

- *Pollution:* Modern herbicide and pesticide sprays are often made with chemicals that endanger wildlife. They can easily drain into waterways and pollute our drinking water. They can also remain on the food crops themselves, endangering the health of those who eat the crops.

*The people of Nepal traditionally use elephant grass to roof their houses. Now more **developed countries** use it for fuel.*

Find out more about these problems. Fossil fuels and rainforest destruction, for instance, are covered at www.rainforestfoundationuk. org and www.rainforestconcern.org. For the problems of increasing food production, look at www.telegraph.co.uk/foodanddrink/7969073/Demand-for-food-is-costing-the-Earth.html.

## What's growing near you?

Do you know what crops are grown in your region? What are they used for? You can find out by going into a **rural** area, looking in fields, and identifying the crops. To help you, use a picture guide such as the *New Oxford Book of Food Plants* (Oxford University Press, 2009). Make sure you keep off private land, and do not cause any damage.

*Corn on the cob is a popular food in many parts of the world.*

## What is cheap food?

Food is the single most important thing we buy. We can survive without cars and televisions and computers, but not without food.

Yet many people expect to pay very little for their food. How does this affect the way food is produced? To meet the demands of consumers, farmers have to grow food as cheaply as possible. This means, for instance, that many chickens and pigs are raised in cramped conditions indoors. Look up 'factory farming' on the internet and you will find plenty of evidence about this.

## Others ways of farming

We have looked at how food is grown today. There are clearly good and bad sides to modern agricultural methods. But is there an alternative? People are coming up with better and more **sustainable** ways of farming, meaning methods that can be continued over time without harming the environment.

New farming ideas are being explored all the time. Here are some of them.

- Farmers can grow crops organically (without using artificial fertilizers and sprays).

### What would YOU do?

Imagine you are a farmer. How are you going to decide on the best way to grow food? The first step is to find out more about different kinds of farming. Start by looking at www.newscientist.com/article/dn19947-we-can-feed-9-billion-people-in-2050.html. Find other sites about alternative growing methods, such as those methods mentioned here. Then make up your mind about how you would do it.

These farm workers are harvesting lettuce grown organically, with no artificial sprays or fertilizers.

- Scientists can develop bigger and better plant varieties by changing the makeup of their genes (the tiny units that give the plants their unique characteristics). These are known as genetically modified (GM) crops.

- Farmers can sow crops without ploughing. This helps the soil to keep **carbon** locked in. The release of carbon in the air is a major cause of **climate change**, meaning the overall change in weather patterns (see page 33).

- Farmers can try permaculture (see box below).

## Permaculture

Permaculture is a sustainable way of farming and living. In contrast to many modern farming methods, permaculture works with nature, not against it. It identifies the local systems found in nature, such as the local weather patterns or insects, and uses them to their best advantage. The aim is to get higher **yields** with less effort by mimicking (copying) nature.

Permaculture extends from agriculture to how we live our everyday lives. On a basic level it can mean recycling and reusing. In broader terms it can mean creating a sustainable community that lives in harmony with nature by not spoiling the local environment, while living off local supplies.

Tomatoes can be planted under plastic sheets, which keep in moisture but stop weeds growing.

# The water crisis

How can there be a water crisis? The world is mostly covered with water. Surely, it seems, there must be plenty for everyone? But the oceans contain only salt water, which we cannot drink or put on crops. We depend on fresh water, which is in much smaller supply. It comes from rivers, lakes, rainfall, and underground wells.

### Water facts

- One in six people throughout the world (1.1 billion total) do not have access to safe drinking water.

- Two in six people (2.6 billion total) do not have proper sanitation because of lack of clean water.

- About 3,900 children die every day from diseases connected with dirty water.

## Who needs water?

We all need water to live, even more so than food. As the planet's **population** rises, so does the demand for fresh water to drink. Water is also needed for other things. Farmers need a lot of water to **irrigate** (get water to) their crops. In fact, some 69 per cent of the available fresh water is used in **agriculture** every year.

Governments and charities are helping to give people reliable water supplies. Since 1990, over 1.6 billion people have gained access to fresh water. But huge numbers still have to go thirsty or suffer from disease because they do not have proper **sanitation** (systems for getting rid of waste).

Vital rice crops in Asia need a lot of water to grow well.

# Drought in Kenya

## Charity appeal: bringing water to Kenya's drought-ridden valleys
### by Sally Williams

'We are crying for rain,' says John Muli, a 57-year-old farmer, as he looks at his seedlings fading fast in the heat.

We are in Kathekani, a village parched by drought in the district of Makueni, south-east Kenya. The deep-red clay has turned to a dust that films over boots, rocks and hubcaps. The maize and beans that once provided Muli with food and school fees are limp.

'If rain doesn't fall I think we will perish,' he says.

This story, published on 3 December 2009, in the *Telegraph*, is about the results of a devastating **drought** that swept across Kenya, in Africa, in 2009. It killed **livestock** (animals raised to provide food or fibres), crops, and people (mainly children).

See if you can find out more about what caused this drought. Look on news websites or on websites of charities such as Oxfam or the Kenya Red Cross. If you do an internet search, type in 'Kenya Drought 2009'. Could the tragedy have been avoided – or not?

Farmers in Kenya dig out a water channel which has become blocked during a drought.

## What causes drought?

During a drought, plants die due to lack of water. As a result, animals, including humans, do not have these plants to eat. Animals and people also need water to drink, and they will die without it.

But what causes drought? There are several natural causes. The most likely is a decrease in rainfall. Without rain, rivers and lakes dry up, and underground wells do not get filled.

Human activity is also a major cause of drought. If we use too much water, the ground will dry out. When we cut down forests, wind and rain can erode (wear away) the rich topsoil. Rain is not held in the bare ground, but rather simply washes away.

## Wasting water

Humans waste a huge amount of precious water in their everyday lives. This happens in our homes – for example, when people leave the tap running while brushing their teeth. It also happens on a much bigger scale in streets, leisure centres, and other areas. Places such as car washes and golf courses use up a lot of water.

## What would YOU do ?

You are probably lucky enough to live in a house where there is water available 24 hours a day. You can turn on a tap for as long as you like. But how much water are you wasting? Saving water can save money. It also helps wildlife by sparing water in rivers and ponds. Think of ways of using less water. Look at www.savingwater. org/kids for some ideas.

If your house has a water meter, use it to keep track of your water usage.

Industries such as farming and manufacturing can also be very wasteful – even when they are making products we all want. Growing, harvesting, and processing materials all use a surprising amount of water. One cup's worth of coffee takes 140 litres (37 gallons) of water to produce. It takes an amazing 2,400 litres (792 gallons) to produce one hamburger.

## A KWL chart

It is easy to get overwhelmed by facts and figures when you are researching a topic. A 'KWL' chart is a simple way of keeping track of what you discover, and for planning ahead. It has three columns: 'What I **K**now', 'What I **W**ant to know', and 'What I **L**earned'. Fill in the first two columns (K and W) before you start, and then fill in the third column (L) as you research.

Here is a filled-in example. The question to answer is: Can farmers cut down water usage?

| What I know | What I want to know | What I learned |
| --- | --- | --- |
| Farmers use a lot of water for their crops. | How can they use less water? | Drip or trickle irrigation for systems are more economical. |

Most fruit and vegetables are thoroughly washed. This uses a lot of water.

## Solutions

How can we work toward making sure everyone has access to clean water and good sanitation? Obviously it would be a good start to cut out all unnecessary waste throughout the world. Money is also needed. Water supply systems can be expensive to install, especially in regions that have little rainfall anyway.

There are many other ways to tackle water shortages. For example:

- *Desalination:* This involves removing the salt from seawater. However, it is very expensive and uses a lot of energy.

- *Rainwater harvesting:* Most rain simply drains into waterways or evaporates (turns into a gas). It can be captured and stored in tanks instead.

- *Domestic meters:* Homes that have water meters tend to use much less water, because people want to save money by using less. But worldwide most households do not have water meters.

- *Reuse of wastewater:* Used water from kitchens, baths, and other sources can be recycled in factories and power plants.

These workers are checking the seawater intake at a desalination plant in Abu Dhabi..

# Water shortages in California

The water crisis has not just hit **developing countries**. In the United States, the state of California suffered a crippling drought beginning in 2007.

In 2009 Governor Arnold Schwarzenegger declared a state of emergency. He ordered all government agencies to use the state's emergency plan for saving water after the third year of drought in a row. 'This drought is having a devastating impact on our people, our communities, our economy, and our environment – making today's action absolutely necessary,' Governor Schwarzenegger said. 'This is a crisis, just as severe as an earthquake or raging wildfire.'

Arnold Schwarzenegger, the governor of California, takes a look at water resources from the air in 2009.

## What would YOU do?

Imagine you are Arnold Schwarzenegger. You have a huge state to govern, and it has not rained heavily for three years. You have to put measures into force that will save water. Do you think water rationing would work? This means only allowing people a limited amount of water per day. Or would this cause problems with industry and farming? How about recycling wastewater? Or bringing it in from other regions?

Look at http://gov.ca.gov/press-release/11556/ for details of what Governor Schwarzenegger did. Also look at www.captainwater.com, a website about water problems in the state of Georgia, USA.

# From farm to plate

Two main things have to happen if we can truly feed the world. Firstly, we need to grow a massive amount of food, so that there is enough for everyone. We know that farmers can do this, even with a rising **population**. Secondly, we need to get the food to hungry people. This is much more difficult.

*Wealthy and stable countries like Japan always have plenty to eat. They can catch fish in the sea, and buy many other kinds of food from abroad.*

## The poverty trap

If your family needs food, someone goes out and buys it. Most of us have money to pay for what we want. So, shops and supermarkets are there to sell us things. Now imagine that you and your neighbours need food, but have no money. You cannot buy anything. In that case, there would be no shops in your area.

**Poverty** is the biggest problem in food **distribution**. Without money, there will be nobody to buy and sell food. The poorest people are often unable to grow food for themselves, because of **drought** or disease. They have no source of food, so they go hungry.

## Politics and war

There are two more major reasons that people lack food and water. One cause is politics. The government of a country, especially in **developing countries**, is in charge of food distribution. Sometimes these leaders are dishonest and keep the food for themselves and their supporters. There is none left for other people.

The second cause is war. Civil wars and conflicts between neighbouring countries bring bloodshed and hardship. They also mean that crops and food shops may be destroyed, and that thousands of people may have to flee from their homes to find safety. A regular supply of food will be very hard to find.

# Somalia

In the African country of Somalia, there has not been a strong government for nearly 20 years. Rival warlords have battled to take control, causing violence and disrupting **agriculture** and **industry**. This has brought on a long-term **famine**. In the early 1990s, 300,000 people in Somalia died because of famine. Since 2009 another drought has caused over two million people to be in serious danger from famine.

Long years of civil war have brought famine and poverty to Somalia.

## Is food for eating – or for selling?

Farmers have a choice. They can grow food that they and their neighbours need for eating. This does not bring them much money, but it ensures they do not go hungry. Or they can grow crops that can be sold abroad for high prices. This brings them money, but it means they still have to buy food for themselves.

Something grown for **export** (selling to another country) is called a **cash crop**. People in **developed countries** buy a lot of cash crops from developing ones. For instance, people in the United Kingdom get coffee from Guatemala, tea from India, and bananas from the West Indies.

## Food is big business

The large food companies encourage the growing of cash crops, which they buy and export. They say that farmers will make a profit from them, which can be used to improve their farms. For these companies, the best crops of all are those that can be preserved and shipped long distances. Why do you think food companies like these kinds of crops?

However, the focus on cash crops can harm the places where they are grown. There may not be enough local food available, and prices may be too high. And is it a good thing for us to be eating food that may have been transported thousands of miles? This uses a lot of energy to drive ships, trucks, and aircraft. It is not the best or most efficient way to distribute food.

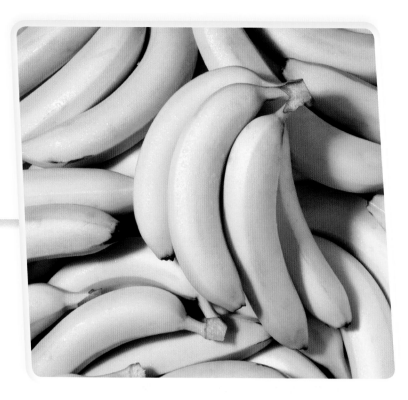

Bananas are one of the most important cash crops in the world.

## Make your own supermarket survey

How far does your food travel? Go to your nearest supermarket and find out. Make a sample selection of different kinds of food (fruits, vegetables, meat, fish, drinks, biscuits, or whatever you like). Then find them on the shelves and look at the labels to see where they were produced. Write the details down in a notebook.

When you get home, you can put your findings in a chart. Use an atlas or the internet to see how far each item has travelled. You could set your chart out like this:

| Food type | Country of origin | Distance travelled (km/miles) |
|---|---|---|
| Ground coffee | Costa Rica | 3,560/2,212 |
| Asparagus | Peru | |
| Tea | India | |
| Canned tuna | Thailand | |

Most of the world's tea is grown in India, China, and other Asian countries.

# Rebuilding communities after civil war

The best way for hungry people to get out of the poverty trap is to grow their own food. Most will need help and advice to do this. For example, southern Sudan, in Africa, has suffered from civil war. Many people fled the area. The few who stayed during the war, and the thousands of **refugees** who are now returning to the area, find it difficult to rebuild their farms and businesses. With no farm animals, seeds, tools, or training, they have to rely on food aid.

However, the land is capable of growing crops. So, small-scale agriculture can help people and their communities to provide their own food. One plan, the FARM-Africa's Southern Sudan Livelihoods Rehabilitation and Development Project, aims to help farmers in practical ways. It is not just giving poor and hungry people food aid, but also helping them to start growing their own food again. Among the aims are:

- training people to dig safe new wells for water
- helping farmers find out the best crops to grow
- providing farm tools, seeds, and **livestock**
- training vets to keep animals healthy.

Villagers in Sudan pump vital water from a newly made well.

## A concept web

A concept web is a visual way of organizing your evidence on a single page. In the middle of the web (like a spider) is the main question. Arrows from this radiate outward, linking to boxes that contain possible answers. More lines branch from these, adding more details – or more questions. For example:

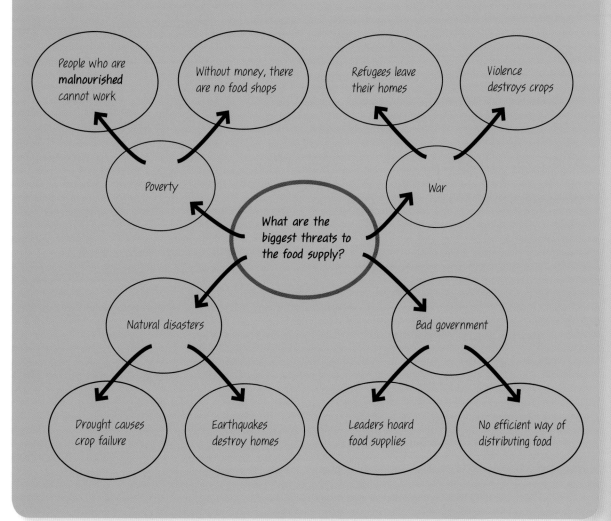

## What would YOU do ?

The supply of food can be cut by many things – wars, dishonest governments, natural disasters, and poverty. But somehow people must be fed. How can you help make sure that food is distributed fairly and regularly? This is a very big question. Start by looking on a website such as www.foodethicscouncil.org.

# Vanishing fields

*'We have let farmland be built upon and ironically it often tends to be the best bits of farmland that are taken.'*

**Jules Pretty, environmentalist and Pro-Vice-Chancellor (Sustainability and Resources), University of Essex, 2009**

If you want to grow crops and raise **livestock**, you need land. Today, enormous areas of the world are used for farming, and more is being cleared every day.

## Cities are spreading ...

Throughout the world, **urban** areas and **industry** are growing fast. Houses, shopping centres, and factories are being built on undeveloped land, most of it once farmland. In the United Kingdom, the loss of farmland to development is continuing, with about 15,000 hectares (37,000 acres) developed from 1996 to 2004.

However, in the United Kingdom, farming still makes up 77 per cent of land use. In **developing countries** that are quickly expanding their economies, such as China, India, and Brazil, the rate of change from farmland to built-up land is speeding up. Land buried beneath buildings and roads may never grow food again.

## ... and so are deserts

A desert is a region so dry that almost no **vegetation** (plants) will grow. The biggest desert in the world is the Sahara Desert in Africa, which covers parts of 11 countries. Since the 1960s, scientists have known that the Sahara is getting bigger, as sand spreads to cover farmland. Other major world deserts are also spreading, and completely new desert areas are appearing.

*Many of the world's deserts, such as the Sahara in Africa, are getting bigger.*

There are several reasons why deserts are expanding. As we burn **fossil fuels** to get energy, they release **carbon** into the air. Carbon and other gases act like the glass in a greenhouse. They trap some of the heat that reaches the Earth from the Sun, preventing it from escaping into space. This is called the greenhouse effect. It is causing global temperatures to rise, a development known as **global warming**. This rise in temperatures leads to changes in weather patterns such as rainfall and wind, which can cause deserts to expand. For some other big reasons for growing deserts, see the chart below.

## How are we helping to destroy farmland?

This chart shows the four main causes of dry land being turned into desert:

- deforestation (cutting down woodland)

- overgrazing (allowing livestock to eat all the vegetation)

- arable farming (ploughing loosens the soil and makes it more likely to wash or blow away)

- bio-industrial usage (over-using chemical **fertilizers**, **herbicides**, and **pesticides**).

This chart shows areas where the land has been badly damaged, or become desert, and how the damage occurred.

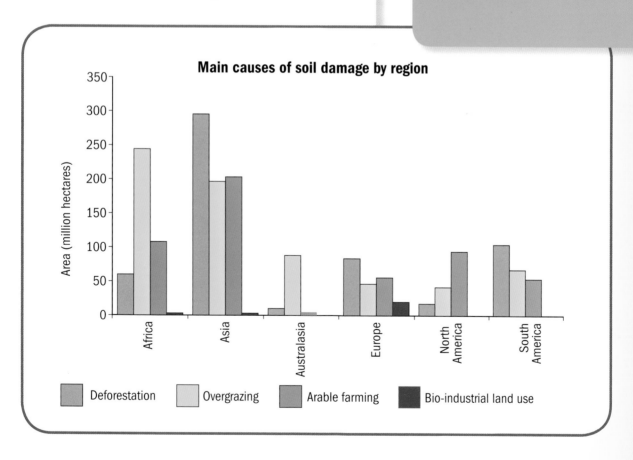

Main causes of soil damage by region

WORD BANK
**global warming**   rising temperatures worldwide, caused by increasing levels of greenhouse gases

## Food deserts

We think of starving people as living in remote **rural** regions. But thousands of people can go hungry in the heart of big cities. They live in 'food deserts', inner-city areas with no food shops in reach. Handicapped, elderly, and poor people cannot get to the distant 'supermarkets'. Their only source of something to eat may be fast food restaurants. Many of these sell foods that have high fat contents and do not offer good **nutrition**. So, these people's diets are likely to make them **obese** (very overweight) and unhealthy.

## Farms without food

Do farmers just grow things we can eat? Of course not. For a start, they grow grass and other plants that their animals can eat. But many farmers grow crops that are not food at all. Some grow cotton or other fibres, which can be turned into clothing. As we have seen, others grow elephant grass and other crops for **biofuel** (see page 16). Crops such as linseed and rapeseed are grown for making chemicals.

*Many urban areas have plenty of fast-food outlets, but no fresh food shops.*

These and many other non-food crops use land that could be growing food. They produce materials that are useful to us – but at a huge cost. Research has shown that growing more biofuels has helped to push up the price of some foods, such as grain. This is because biofuels themselves can be sold at high prices. Perhaps the best way of saving our farmland for food crops is to research alternatives to fossil fuels or biofuels. We could also try to use less of everything, particularly in **developed countries** in the West.

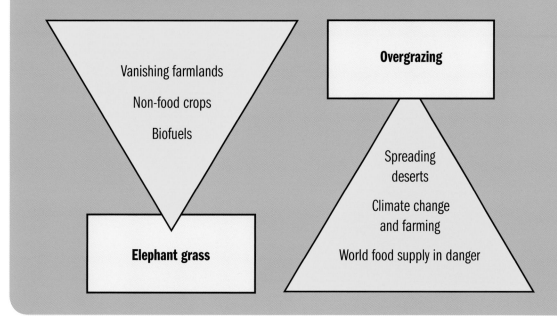

## Use a triangle chart

It can be confusing to research a topic that is big or complex. Use a triangle chart to narrow it down. Put your topic, vanishing farmlands, at the top of the triangle. Underneath, write down keywords that focus on a smaller research area, like the example on the left.

Or you can broaden a topic out. Simply turn the triangle the other way.

Vanishing farmlands

Non-food crops

Biofuels

**Elephant grass**

**Overgrazing**

Spreading deserts

Climate change and farming

World food supply in danger

## China's silk trade

Silk is one of China's most famous products. It is made by silkworms, which feed on mulberry leaves. Today, food for silkworms seems to be limiting the growth of food for humans. As a result, the people of China do not have as much farmland. Is this right? **Exports** of silk earn a lot of money for China. What is better for a developing economy like China's – having more money or more food?

Cotton is a major non-food crop in the United States.

## Grabbing land

Are you worried about future food supplies? Are you very rich? If so, you can simply buy up the rights to farmland in other countries. This is what is happening in some parts of the world today. Wealthy governments and businesses are making land deals with poorer ones. For example, investors from oil-rich countries in the Middle East are buying farmland in Sudan, Ukraine, Pakistan, and Thailand.

Many people see these land grabs as a threat to a country's **food security**. With foreign owners, local farmers will lose control of their crops. Developing countries could end up growing food for rich ones, instead of feeding their own hungry populations.

## Dealing with it

How can we stop our farmlands and other important areas in nature from disappearing? Here are some ideas for solving these very big problems.

- *Spreading cities:* Urban development could be controlled much more tightly. There should only be new building on 'brownfield' (already-used) sites, rather than 'greenfield' (unused) ones.

- *Global warming:* As we have seen (see page 33), global warming is largely caused by the burning of fossil fuels such as coal and oil. If we switch to other types of energy, such as nuclear power, solar (Sun) power, wind power, or hydroelectric (water) power, we could release less carbon.

- *Desertification:* Desertification is when an area where crops or plants once grew dries out and can no longer allow most things to grow. Better livestock management could prevent overgrazing. Areas in danger of becoming desert could be planted with trees and other suitable vegetation to keep moisture in the soil and stop it from blowing away.

*The Chinese are planting thousands of young trees to stop the Gobi Desert from spreading.*

- *Non-food crops:* Obviously, we are always going to need natural fibres such as cotton and silk. But are biofuel crops really necessary? Scientists are already developing other ways of producing artificial fuels that do not need farmland, including the growth of special algae.

- *Foreign buyers:* The investment of money by a rich country can help a poor one, as long as the deal is carefully controlled. Otherwise, people can put pressure on their governments to refuse bad deals.

## What would YOU do ?

Look at the problems and possible solutions on these pages. You can find out a lot more about each of the topics mentioned here in books or on the internet (start by looking up 'climate change and farming'). Now make your mind up. Should farmland be preserved? If so, how would you do it?

It is very important that traditional rice paddy fields, like these in Madagascar, are preserved so that local people have the food that they need.

# We want good food

We have seen that millions of people throughout the world never have enough to eat. But there is more to our diet than simply having enough food. The food should also be healthy and full of **nutrients**.

## What is good food?

Eating good food keeps us fit and strong. It helps us to fight off illness and to have energy for work. But how do we know what is good? For a start, good food is safe food. It should be clean and as fresh as possible. Dirty or stale food can spread disease.

Good food should be part of a properly mixed diet. Human bodies work best on a combination of different kinds of food:

- **starchy** foods (such as rice, bread, potatoes, or pasta)
- fresh fruit and vegetables
- **protein**-rich foods (such as eggs, beans, fish, or meat)
- dairy products (such as cheese or yogurt).

## The effects of malnutrition

Of course, most hungry people do not have a choice. They are glad to have any food at all. But in **famine**-stricken regions, this food is likely to be scarce and low in quality. Food will not have enough vitamins or proteins to help bodies grow. The result is lack of proper **nutrition** – people are **malnourished**.

*People and cattle go hungry during a **drought** in Niger.*

People who starve or eat bad food over a long period suffer in many ways. Their bodies do not grow properly, so they are always small and weak. Malnourished babies are much more likely to die young than well-fed ones. Those who survive are more likely to have diseases or mental problems.

## How can we help?

Millions of starving people depend on charities to give them food. But this food has to be nutritious. A lot of food aid consists of flour and other starchy foods. Malnourished people (especially children) need much more than that. Some charities are able to open emergency clinics where children are fed with food that has vitamins and minerals added to it.

Charities that provide food clearly need support and money from people in **developed countries**. However, sending food is not the best solution to this tragic problem. Hungry people need to be helped to produce their own food, or to earn enough money to buy it. Look back through the book and make a list of the changes that have to be made to give everyone a fair supply of food and water.

Farmers in Nicaragua receive government help to look after their crops.

## Too much food?

Although some parts of the world suffer from food shortages, others have more than enough. And many people in these areas tend to eat too much. Today, there are over one billion overweight people on Earth, and more than 300 million of these people are classified as **obese**.

The word *obese* means that the fat content in a person's body has reached dangerous levels. Obesity is caused by eating too many fatty foods and not getting enough exercise. Obese people are more likely to die young and to suffer from cancer and many other diseases.

### The ten most overweight countries

Here are the countries with the largest **populations** in the world that are overweight, according to surveys by the World Health Organization compiled between 2000 and 2008.

| Rank | Country | Percentage of population |
|------|---------|--------------------------|
| 1. | American Samoa | 93.5 |
| 2. | Kiribati (Pacific Ocean) | 81.5 |
| 3. | United States | 66.7 |
| 4. | Germany | 66.5 |
| 5. | Egypt | 66.0 |
| 6. | Bosnia-Herzegovina | 62.9 |
| 7. | New Zealand | 62.7 |
| 8. | Israel | 61.9 |
| 9. | Croatia | 61.4 |
| 10. | United Kingdom | 61.0 |

You can find out more about global obesity by looking at the website of the World Health Organization, at www.who.int/mediacentre/factsheets/fs311/en/index.html.

## Eating can kill

Just because you have plenty of food, that does not mean you will be healthy. For a start, it can make you obese. Food can also be bad for your health in other ways. Many modern foods are processed, meaning they have been changed from their natural state – for example, in order to be canned. Processed foods contain large amounts of sugar, salt, and fats. They can also contain other substances that are harmful to our bodies.

People who eat too much fatty or salty food can suffer big health problems.

People who eat too much of these 'bad' foods have a high risk of suffering from diabetes, heart disease, and cancer, as well as many less serious illnesses. In fact, you could say they were malnourished – just like those people who are harmed by long-term hunger.

## What would YOU do ?

Do you eat good food? Make a survey of what you and your family eat throughout the week. Find out what ingredients each kind of processed food contains by reading the details on the package (you may need to ask an adult for help). You could set out your record like this:

| Date (time) | Type of food | Starch | Protein | Sugar | Salt | Fat |
|---|---|---|---|---|---|---|
| 10/12 (8.00) | Orange juice | 26g | 2g | 22g | 0g | 0g |
| | Cereal | 25g | 3g | 8g | 0.2g | 1.5g |
| | Milk | 12g | 8g | 12g | 0.12g | 5g |

Think of ways to make your diet healthier. Start by looking at the eatwell plate on the NHS Choices website. This tells you how much of each sort of food you should try to eat from the eatwell plate.

# What we all eat

What do you eat? Are you a vegetarian or a meat-eater? Is your diet different from that of the rest of your family? Or your neighbours? What do people eat on the other side of your town or city? Or on the other side of the world?

Take a look at the sample tables on these pages and then create your own. The first table – 'What I eat' – is where you can list the foods you eat in all the different categories (fruit, vegetables, dairy products, and so on). A staple food is the one that forms the basis of what you eat, or the thing you have the most of—for example, bread or rice.

The second table, 'What the world eats', will give you a little more work to do. You need to find out and list what people eat in other regions of the world. Can you think of more headings for food groups you could add – for example, 'pulses', 'sweets' or 'drinks'? Maybe you can try out some of their foods.

## What I eat

| Staple food | Vegetables | Fruits | Meat | Fish |
|---|---|---|---|---|
| bread | potatoes | apples | beef | tuna |
| wheat | peas | oranges | bacon | salmon |
| pasta | onions | bananas | chicken | cod |
| rice | carrots | grapes | | |

| Pulses | Dairy | Sweets | Drinks |
|---|---|---|---|
| lentils | milk | chocolate | juice |
| beans | cheese | biscuits | cola |
| chickpeas | butter | cake | tea |
| | yogurt | cereal | |

# What the world eats

| | Staple food | Vegetables | Fruits | Meat | Fish | Dairy | (Heading?) | (Heading?) |
|---|---|---|---|---|---|---|---|---|
| South and Central America | | | | | | | | |
| Northern Europe | | | | | | | | |
| Southern Europe | | | | | | | | |
| Middle East | | | | | | | | |
| Central Asia | | | | | | | | |
| East Asia | | | | | | | | |
| South Asia | | | | | | | | |
| South East Asia | | | | | | | | |
| Australasia | | | | | | | | |
| Northern Africa | | | | | | | | |
| Southern Africa | | | | | | | | |

# Glossary

**agriculture** farming

**biofuel** crop grown so that it can be processed and used as a fuel, either in a power station or to power a vehicle

**carbon** one of the most common elements, which occurs in many forms. It can combine with oxygen (another element) to form carbon dioxide. This is one of the main gases that cause global warming.

**cash crop** crop that is grown to be sold, rather than for eating locally

**climate change** change in the temperature, rainfall, or wind caused by human activity

**developed country** country that has a stable way of organizing its money, goods, and trade

**developing country** country that does not yet have a stable way of organizing its money, goods, and trade

**distribution** spreading or delivering of something over a wide area

**drought** severe and long-lasting lack of water in a region

**export** sell and transport something to another country

**famine** extreme food shortage

**fertilizer** special material spread on the ground to help plants grow better

**food security** having a reliable food source

**fossil fuel** fuel, such as coal, oil, or natural gas, that was formed by the decay of ancient plants and animals

**global warming** rising temperatures worldwide, caused by increasing levels of greenhouse gases

**herbicide** chemical that is sprayed on the ground to destroy unwanted plants (such as weeds)

**industry** type of work that creates something to be sold, often through the use of factories and power plants

**irrigate** spray or channel water to crops to help them grow

**livestock** animals raised by farmers to provide food or fibres (such as wool)

**malnourished** lacking essential nutrients in one's diet, which results in disease and other difficulties

**nutrient** substance in food that supports health and growth

**nutrition** consumption of food that helps bodies to grow and replace their tissues (such as bone)

**obese** describes a person whose body has a fat content that has reached dangerous levels

**pesticide** chemical that is sprayed on the ground to destroy animal and insect pests that harm crops

**pollution** harming the environment with poisonous or dangerous substances

**population** total number of people in an area

**poverty** state of being poor, with little money and few ways to support oneself

**protein** substance that helps the body grow and repair itself

**refugee** person forced to leave his or her home to find a new place to live, because of war or natural disaster

**rural** relating to the countryside

**sanitation** system for getting rid of sewage and other waste

**starch** substance found in foods such as bread and potatoes that gives the body energy to burn up

**sustainable** when resources are managed so that they will not run out in the future, causing little damage to the environment

**United Nations (UN)** organization of different countries that formed in 1945 to promote world peace and security

**urban** relating to a city

**vegetation** plants that cover an area of land

**yield** amount of food produced

# Find out more

## Books

*Feeding the World* (Food and Farming), Richard and Louise Spilsbury (Wayland, 2009)

*Feeding the World* (Headline Issues), Sarah Levete (Heinemann Library, 2010)

*Follow that Food: distribution of resources* (Fusion), Buffy Silverman, 2007)

*Graphing Food and Nutrition* (Real World Data), Isabel Thomas (Heinemann Library, 2007)

*Graphing Water* (Real World Data), Sarah Medina (Heinemann Library, 2007)

*Planning for a Sustainable Future* (Geography Skills), Helen Belmont (Franklin Watts, 2007)

*Running Water* (Geography Focus), Louise Spilsbury (Raintree, 2007)

*The Pros and Cons of Water Power* (Energy Debates), Louise and Richard Spilsbury (Wayland, 2007)

*Water for Everyone* (Headline Issues), Sarah Levete (Heinemann Library, 2010)

## Websites

Many useful websites are mentioned throughout the text of this book. Here are a few more.

www.streetchildafrica.org.uk/pages/new-years-resolution.html
Visit the website of the charity Street Child Africa to learn how children in Africa are being helped to provide food and water for themselves and their families.

www.build-africa.org
This charity helps young Africans escape poverty through education

www.irinnews.org
IRIN is a news agency run by the United Nations. Find out the latest news about global problems like hunger and drought on its website.

www.oxfam.org.uk
The charity Oxfam has a wide-ranging website about fighting poverty and hunger.

www.wfp.org
The website of the UN's World Food Program is full of interesting information.

www.worldtoilet.org
Get involved on World Toilet Day celebrate the importance of sanitation and raise awareness for the 2.5 billion people who don't have access to toilets and proper sanitation

www.worldwaterrelief.org
The organization World Water Relief is dedicated to bringing everyone clean water.

## DVDs

**Super Size Me** (2004)
This documentary charts the health dangers of eating fast food.

**Foodmatters** (2009)
This documentary is about the effect that modern processed food is having on our health.

**One Man, One Cow, One Planet** (2008)
A documentary showing how farmers on poor soils can grow better crops without chemicals.

**Our Daily Bread** (2005)
How is your food really produced? This film shows you in graphic images, but without spoken commentary.

**The Future of Food** (2007)
This hard-hitting film is about the development and dangers of genetically modified (GM) crops.

# Index